Y0-EKS-909

Katherin...
what ... ...le
one of my ...
in the world that ... ...nd
of myself. Happy Bir...
take good care of yourself.

Tom Zimmer...
April, 1989

WORKING AT THE STADIUM

WORKING AT THE STADIUM

Dodger Players, Fans, and Vendors in a Championship Season

Photographs and Text
by
Tom Zimmerman

Pacific Tides Press
Los Angeles

Copyright © 1989 by Tom Zimmerman
All rights reserved.
Except for brief quotations for review, no part of this
book may be reproduced in any form without written
permission from the publisher.

Pacific Tides Press
Post Office Box 67621
Los Angeles, California 90067

Library of Congress Catalog Card Number:
89—90779

ISBN 0-9622013-0-8

First Edition

Dedicated to my father
Pius Zimmerman
And the memory of my mother
Catherine Albrecht Zimmerman

ACKNOWLEDGEMENTS

Working at the Stadium started as a series of articles for the *Los Angeles Downtown News*. Marc Porter Zasada is every writer's dream editor. He has the most wonderful habit of saying, "Hum. Yeah, I like it," to most of my ideas.

Once I got the go ahead from the *News*, the Dodgers were very helpful. The entire organization was very patient with answering questions and ignoring the camera. Particularly helpful was Ruth Ruiz. When the book reached its final stages, Michael Vizvary always managed to track down even the most arcane pieces of information.

Anyone who knows Nancy Newman Work appreciates her impeccable taste and design sense. I am lucky enough to know her very well and have been the grateful recipient of her insight, trust, and cheerleading. It has helped more than words are capable of conveying, but this book is much better for all the advice and encouragement she gives me.

I was also helped by many words of wisdom and warning from Michael John Sullivan. He was always ready to give a supportive word when one was most needed. Another source of great help in translating my ideas and visions to the printed page was Gary Collins.

I learned about history before I did photography. For their instruction, I am grateful to Anthony Turhollow of Loyola-Marymount University, and Thomas Hines and Norris Hundley of UCLA.

My father, Pius Zimmerman, first taught me how to use a camera. My brother, Paul, and friend, T.G. Lane helped refine these first lessons. Over the years, Mike Tandy (owner of the legendary Art Craft Rental Darkroom), Larry Calderon, Lee Romero, Barbara Gold, and Mitzi Landau all helped me learn my art. Rachel Lozzi, my representative, has been both insightfully critical and strongly supportive.

I was very fortunate in that all the baseball coaches I ever had never did anything to quell my love for the game. Particular thanks go to Burt Kearns. My parents always encouraged an interest in baseball, even when it came to putting up with the constant sight of me listening to Vin Scully and Jerry Doggett on an old white radio while supposedly trying to do home work.

Finally, I want to thank Sr. Colette McManus for eleven years of Job-like patience.

Tom Zimmerman
Los Angeles

TABLE OF CONTENTS

Forward—page 10

Introduction: Professional Baseball in Los Angeles—page 12

I   Pre-Game—page 22

II   The Game—page 60

III   Post-Game—page 90

Afterward—Dodger Day Downtown—page 116

A Los Angeles Baseball Bibliography—page 118

Working at the Stadium is a celebration of a day spent at Dodger Stadium. It wanders from the field to vendor's booths, stopping for a hot dog along the way. The day starts with the timeless, echoing sound of a wooden bat hitting a ball in an empty Stadium. It ends with the high pitched whine of air blowers cleaning the place up after tens of thousands of people have passed through and gone.

Part of the story is the Dodger organization. Its competence is a staple of any story dealing with the team or the Stadium. There is no better environment for watching a baseball game than Dodger Stadium. Bob Wood's *From Dodger Dogs to Fenway Franks* is a book length investigation of the ambience of the 26 Major League ballparks. He grades each of them on subjects such as appearance, food quality, employee friendliness, and upkeep. After visiting every park in both leagues, Wood decided Dodger Stadium and Royals Stadium in Kansas City were tied for first place. He described the Dodgers' home as "the most stately structure in the game today."

But as beautiful as the ballpark might be, fans buy tickets to see the team play. In the 31 seasons since the team came west, the World Championship pennant has fluttered in the center field breeze at Dodger Stadium on five separate occasions. The team has had eleven first place finishes and nine in second place. There have been fallow periods, but they never last long. Minor leaguers graduate to the majors, trades are made, free agents are acquired. Soon the team is back in contention.

As anyone who has ever spent any time thinking about popular culture knows, there is more to be learned from sports than who won and why. Professional athletics—or television, films, and literature—tells us a lot about the society that both produces and enjoys them. The reaction of Los Angeles fans to Kirk Gibson and his aggressiveness offers insights into this most misunderstood of cities. Perceptions of Dodger manager Tommy Lasorda are indicative of the role expectations assigned to American men. The autograph seekers around the players' parking lot after the game are part of the nationwide yearning to play some sort of role in the lives of the nation's idols.

The most striking thing about watching professional athletes close up is seeing the tiger they all must ride. It is an animal made up in equal parts of talent, competition, and desire. All three are necessary to make the beast whole, and its hunger is never satiated. There are only 26 major league teams with space for 24 players each. The minor leagues are full of thousands of prospects desperate to take their place on the big club. The competition between those on the inside, and the aggressive horde on the outside is intense. Intense and unceasing.

The concentration and aggression that fuels the drive to reach the majors cannot be shut off just because a man reaches his late 30s and can no longer summon the skills that were his such a short time before. It seems to take years to tame the tiger. To convince the animal that it was a nice ride while it lasted, but now it is over. It was particularly interesting in talking to former players in their new, nonplaying baseball roles to see who had the tiger caged, and who is still holding the reins, eager for just one more chance to ride.

The Los Angeles Dodgers have been a wildly successful franchise. The main reason for this is the nature of the organization. Poor team showing has always brought shakeups. Not in management, but on the field where it will do some good. One family has owned the team since it left Brooklyn. The ballpark is scrupulously tended. All major factors in running a prosperous organization. But it should not be forgotten that the Dodgers were the beneficiary of a long tradition of support for professional baseball by Los Angeles fans.

PACIFIC COAST LEAGUE

The dust was just settling from the first of Los Angeles' many real estate booms when the city fielded its first professional baseball team. It was the late 1880s, and the streets were only just starting to be paved in the obscure town in Southern California. The team was a part of the outlaw California League—a circuit that was not recognized by the National Association of Professional Baseball Clubs. Home games were played at Praeger and Chutes Parks. They were part of a large amusement center located south of downtown where Hill St. dead ended into Washington Blvd. The 19th century team's chief claims to fame are a night game played in 1893 which was lit by 20 kerosene lamps suspended on wires between poles, and that future evangelist Billy Sunday was a starting center fielder.

Oranized baseball first came to Los Angeles when the Pacific Coast League opened for business in 1903. The city's entry was called the Angels, and would remain one of the mainstays of the AAA League until the Dodgers came west in 1958. The Angeles' first seasons were played at Chutes Park, later switching to nearby Washington Park.

Former Coast League great, Jimmie Reese, currently entering his 66th year in professional baseball as a coach with the California Angels, played in Washington Park as a second baseman with the Oakland Oaks. He remembers it as a typical minor league ballpark of its time. All the fencing and the single tiered grandstand was made of wood. If you threw in the standing room, there was a capacity of maybe 15,000 fans.

The Angels were one of the anchors of the P.C.L. for the next half century. The second local entry in the League has a much more traveled history. The team started life as the Vernon Tigers in 1909 when the P.C.L. expanded to accommo-

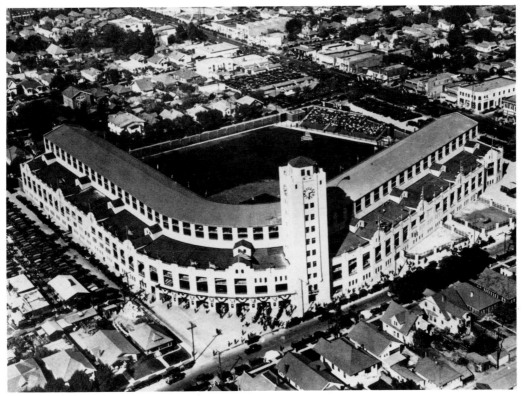

Wrigley Field, c. 1930

date a Sacramento franchise. The Tigers represented Vernon from 1909 to 1912 and again from 1915 to 1925. The two missing years were spent in Venice. After sixteen years of marginal success, the team moved north to join the Seals in San Francisco, changing their name to the Missions. Thirteen years later, after being the second team in a major city again, the Missions came back to Los Angeles as the second edition of the Hollywood Stars. In a foreshadowing of the Dodgers in 1958, the "Twinks" (as in "twinkle, twinkle little star") played their first season at Gilmore Stadium, a converted football field.

WRIGLEY FIELD

In 1921, William Wrigley, Jr., who owned a chewing gum company, most of the Chicago Cubs, and all of Santa Catalina Island, bought the Los Angeles Angels from Johnny Powers. He soon found himself at odds with the city government. Mirroring a similar dilemma that would confront Walter O'Malley in Brooklyn some 35 years later, Wrigley argued that his team's fans could not reach the ballpark by car since parking was so inadequate. Washington Park was primarily served by streetcars, and in 1921 Angelenos were already deeply engrossed in their continuing affair with the automobile. Wrigley wanted to put in underground parking. The city said no, so he decided to move.

Land was purchased south of the central city at 42nd and Avalon Blvd. and the nation's second Wrigley Field was constructed. The Los Angeles ballpark was a slightly scaled down version of the original in Chicago. Like its eastern counterpart it was easily reached by interurban train and the ball carried well when the wind was blowing out. The brick outfield wall was lightly covered with ivy and there was a small center field bleacher section under a huge scoreboard.

There were a few differences. This was Southern California in the early 1920s, after all. Tile covered the roof of both the grandstand and the office tower and palm trees grew just beyond the outfield fences. The dimensions were somewhat smaller than the major league park. Angel batters were faced with 340 foot foul lines and a center field wall 412 feet away. But the power alleys were only 345 feet. These friendly dimensions helped make the western edition as much a paradise for fans of offensive baseball as its eastern counterpart. One very large difference existed between the two Wrigley Fields. Lights for night time baseball were added in Los Angeles in 1930.

Wrigley Field was officially unveiled on September 29, 1925. The Commissioner of Baseball,

Judge Kenesaw Mountain Landis, took the train west to officiate at the ceremonies. The ballpark, like its two year old neighbor, the Coliseum, was dedicated as a memorial to America's veterans of the First World War. The chewing gum magnate spared no expense in making the stadium the class of the Pacific Coast League. Wrigley Field was the only venue in the circuit that had a concrete grandstand until Seals Stadium opened in San Francisco six years later. Jimmie Reese did not see a better place to play ball until he went up to the New York Yankees in 1930.

Some great baseball was played at Wrigley over the years. The field was in almost continuous use during the season once the Angels were joined at the park from 1926 to 1935 by the first edition of the Hollywood Stars. Two legendary California natives sharpened their skills here before their inevitable graduation to the majors. San Francisco's Joe DiMaggio went right from the sandlots to AAA play with the Seals before going on the the Yankees. Ted Williams went directly from Hoover High School in San Diego to the P.C.L. Padres and quickly on to the Red Sox. Such stellar players obviously brought fans to the ballparks but the backbone of the League was the players that excelled at the AAA level but never quite made it into the big leagues. Two Angels are prominant in this category. Jigger Statz played centerfield for the Angels in the 1920s and '30s. He holds the Coast League records for most put outs, assists, chances accepted, and season fielding percentage. Steve Bilko came to the Angels in the mid-1950s after several seasons with the St. Louis Browns and Cardinals. Wrigley Field could have been built with Bilko in mind. He hit 55 home runs in 1956 and 56 home runs in 1957, giving Angel fans something to cheer about in the team's final two seasons.

Wrigley Field was one of the larger parks in the P.C.L. and could accommodate 22,000 fans. This generally provided far more seats than were necessary. Former usher, Bill Fitzgerald, remembers counting 136 people in the park one cold day in 1947. But all of them were full for important games such as the League Championship series and big games with cross town rivals, the Hollywood Stars.

Another sure filler of chairs was the arrival of major league barnstormers. Such teams came by in October and November after the close of the big league season. Teams would usually be led by a name star—such as Ty Cobb, Rogers Hornsby, Babe Ruth, or Bob Feller—and would consist of players from various major or AAA teams who wanted to make some extra money in the days when even a major leaguer needed a second job to make ends meet. The competition was keen and the crowds large whenever big league stars came to Los Angeles, but never more so than when one of the teams was made up of stars from the Negro Leagues. Satchel Paige often headed these teams of players barred from participation in "organized" baseball because of race until Branch Rickey signed Jackie Robinson to play for the Dodgers Montreal farm club in 1946.

Both Wrigley Field and the Angels were purchased by the Brooklyn Dodgers in 1956. After officially agreeing to move west in 1957, the Major League team set up its offices at Wrigley. The Giants played their home games at Seals Stadium in San Francisco until the unfortunate Candlestick Park opened in 1961, but Wrigley was deemed too small for major league play by Dodger brass. So the team played at the jerry rigged Coliseum for the next four years.

No professional teams played at Wrigley between 1958 and 1960, but the old park did show up periodically on television. Both "Home Run Derby" and "The Mighty Casey" episode from the "Twilight Zone" were filmed there. In 1961, an American League expansion team, called appropriately the Los Angeles Angels, played its first season at Wrigley Field. But the following year the team moved to Dodger Stadium, which they called Chavez Ravine Stadium, while their own ballpark was being built in Anaheim. In 1966 the team went south to become the California Angels.

With its Pacific Coast League team in Spokane and its American League team in Anaheim, Wrigley Field's days were numbered. After several years of housing soft ball leagues and traveling carnivals, Wrigley Field was dismantled. Gilbert Lindsay park now occupies the old corner at 42nd and Avalon.

GILMORE FIELD
When Bob Cobb, president of the Brown Derby Restaurants, led a group bid to buy the Hollywood club from San Francisco beer baron, Herbert Fleischaker, in 1938, he was determined to give the Stars a home park separate from Wrigley Field. In order to raise the necessary capital to build the new stadium on Gilmore Island at Beverly and Fairfax and pay operating expenses, Cobb sold blocks of stock in the club. Among the takers were several people prominant in Hollywood's chief local industry. Gary Cooper, George Raft, Robert Taylor, Barbara Stanwyck, Cecil B. DeMille, Bing Crosby, George Burns, Gracie Allen, and William Powell all had a piece of the club. This close association with Holly-

Gilmore Field, 1939

wood celebrities would be one of the lasting hallmarks of Gilmore Field.

The new home of the Hollywood Stars was a more traditional minor league park than Wrigley. It had a wooden grandstand with seating for 12,987 fans. Eucalyptus trees sprouted behind the advertising covered outfield fence, not bleachers. The small foul territory tended to put the fans right on top of the action. Gilmore was 335 feet down the foul lines and 400 feet to dead center. The intimacy of the park also gave fans a chance to check the movie stars who often attended. Former Twink first baseman, Chuck Stevens, notes that casting directors also came to Gilmore. He played small parts in several movies, including the Warner Bros. epic, "Grover Cleveland Alexander," starring ex-baseball broadcaster, Ronald Reagan. Stevens' friend, Hall of Famer Bob Lemon, was Reagan's stand-in for the long shots of "Alexander" pitching.

The post-war Stars were a power house team. Under Fred Haney and Bobby Bragan they were league champs in 1949, 1952, and 1953. Their president, Bob Cobb, was instrumental in trying to build up the P.C.L. so it could eventually become a third major league. This met with scant interest from the American and National Leagues, of course. The stronger the rumors became of a bona fide Major League team coming to Los Angeles, the less interest anyone had in gradually developing a new league.

The final straw came when CBS purchased the land under Gilmore Field and nearby Gilmore Stadium (used for football and midget car racing). The land was earmarked for the network's west coast television headquarters. Notice was served to the Stars that their home field would be razed in 1958. Bob Cobb had hoped to move his team elsewhere in the Los Angeles area before it was announced that the Dodgers were definitely coming. He had been looking at land in the San Fernando Valley but was particularly attracted to a large parcel of land adjacent to downtown called Chavez Ravine.

THE DODGERS HEAD WEST
The Dodgers move to the West Coast is basically a story of one city that was desperate to get a major league team and very aggressive in luring one, and another city that could never organize itself sufficiently to keep its two National League franchises.

Los Angeles had been in the market for a big league club since the St. Louis Browns planned move west was interrupted by World War II. The city had plenty of empty land and was willing to use it as a bargaining chip. On the other coast,

Walter O'Malley, principal stockholder of the Brooklyn Dodgers, had been telling New York officials for years that Ebbets Field no longer filled the bill. The Brooklyn ballpark and its manic fans occupy a favored place in the imagination of all baseball fans. But in point of fact, by the mid-1950s the park was in desperate need of repair, had almost no automobile parking, was served by only one subway line, found itself in a rapidly deteriorating neighborhood, and suffered from declining attendance. O'Malley wanted to build a new stadium at Atlantic and Flatbush in Brooklyn, which would have alleviated all of Ebbets Field's problems. This proposal was rejected. The best the city of New York would offer was the possibility of using some land in Flushing Meadows in Queens. It wasn't as far away as Los Angeles, but this still would have taken the team out of Brooklyn.

While the eastern city was delaying and telling O'Malley that none of his plans were feasible, Los Angeles, in the persons of Mayor Norris Poulson and his representatives, was doing everything in its power to lure the team to the other side of the continent. Land for a new stadium and millions of potential fans were the city's major chips.

Three other factors entered the equation. The 50 year old homology of the major leagues ended in 1953 when the Braves left Boston for Milwaukee. The results were dramatic. Attendance rose from 281,278 in Boston to 1,826,397 in Milwaukee. Technology also played a role. Transcontinental jet passenger planes were just coming into service in 1957, making the long trip west feasible both in terms of time and cost. The third factor was that the Dodgers were not headed west alone. Their old cross town rivals, the Giants were going along.

The Dodgers officially announced their decision to move to Los Angeles on October 7, 1957. The major lure was the Chavez Ravine. The Dodgers wanted to build the stadium themselves, but they needed a city to condemn the land. It would take two years of court cases before the transfer of the Ravine to the Dodgers would take place. The area had originally been a pleasant, semi-urban neighborhood of haphazardly arranged homes. All that was changed when it was renewed with a typical post-war vengeance starting in 1949. The old homes were flattened, the people moved out. A federally subsidized housing project called Elysian Park Heights was slated to rise on the site. This plan was condemned as creeping socialism in the Red Scare era of the early 1950s, and the city council voted to shelve the project in 1952. So when the city went looking for a place to offer the Dodgers as a ballpark site, Chavez Ravine was already largely vacant due to the abandoned plan for public housing.

While the courts were deciding just who had title to Chavez Ravine, the Dodgers set up shop in the Los Angeles Memorial Coliseum. This venerable stadium had been built in 1923 and was later expanded for the 1932 Olympics. In its time, it has hosted lots of football games, political and religious conventions, the celebration of the 150th anniversary of Los Angeles cityhood, two Olympics, and several Bruce Springsteen concerts, but it made a lousy baseball park.

Still, Dodger management was nothing if not creative. The only way to fit a baseball diamond in the Coliseum was to make the right field foul line a cozy 300 feet and the left field line an absurd 251 feet. Center field zoomed out to 420 feet, with power alleys 375 to 400 feet from home plate. To compensate for the minuscule distance to left, a 42 foot high screen was erected that ran 140 feet along the left field fence. It was the same idea as Fenway Park in Boston — short field, tall wall. Only at the Coliseum people had to sit behind it so the fence was a wire screen. Sportswriters dubbed it the "Chinese screen." Dodger outfielder, Wally Moon, rear-

ranged his left-handed swing and became famous for his "Moon shots" that were popped over the nearby wall. Pitchers referred to such blooper home runs as "screeno jobs."

The Dodger sojourn at the Coliseum lasted four years. While the team played baseball, management and city government were faced with a refendum on the transfer of ownership of Chavez Ravine to the Dodgers. The vote on June 3, 1958 was a narrow victory for the team. It would be another year and four months until a Supreme Court decision finalized the city's promises to the Dodgers as legal. Groundbreaking had taken place on September 17, 1959 while the appeal was still before the Court. With the final hurdle cleared, the bulldozers gathered in earnest. It would take two and one half years and the movement of eight million cubic yards of earth to recontour the washes and gullies of Chavez Ravine into the ballpark envisioned by Walter O'Malley and his architect, Emil Praeger.

The official transfer of land involved trading the Chavez Ravine land for the Wrigley Field property. The city built the roads into the new park, but the Dodgers built the Stadium itself- with their own money. This used to be the common method of building ballparks, but today, Dodger Stadium is the only privately owned park in the major leagues.

Certainly the resulting ballpark was worth the wait. Dodger Stadium was been a hit with fans ever since the first game was played against the Cincinnati Reds on April 10, 1962. The seats are comfortable, the sight lines unobstructed, the feeling intimate and spacious at the same time. The place was pretty bare in 1962 but the trees and shrubs have slowly grown to create a park like atmosphere as you approach the Stadium from the acres of parking lots.

Sitting in the Top Deck General Admission seats, you can look out beyond the Pavilion seats to the rolling hills of Southern California. Turning around, you get the best view of Downtown Los Angeles available anywhere in the city. Dodger Stadium affords the fan not only a wonderful place to see a baseball game, but also the perfect representation of the nature of our national pastime—the sublime combination of our rural past with our urban present.

The desire to be a major league city helped bring the Dodgers to Los Angeles. For its part, the main lure to the team was all those fans and the chance to build a dream ballpark. Dodger Stadium is now the third oldest park in the National League. But with the meticulous care showered on it, the Stadium should go on playing host to fans for decades to come.

PRE-GAME

It is noon on a game day at Dodger Stadium. The coaches won't start arriving for another two and a half hours, the players for another three. The press box is empty. Its denizens won't be here until 5:00 or so. The gates won't be open to the fans for an hour after that. It is seven and a half hours until game time. At noon the Stadium is largely empty. But not completely.

The Dodger offices scattered throughout the park are busy planning everything from future group visits, to how many hot dogs to order for the next homestand, or possible trades to strengthen the team. Up on the Club Level, a maintenance man is repairing one of the seats. On the field the grounds keepers are at work sculpting the playing field. Outside the Stadium, gardeners are seeing to the shrubbery that surrounds the ballpark. Somewhere else in the complex a video technician is checking his equipment, making certain it will be ready for the night's game.

The pace picks up considerably when the team gets ready for batting practice. This is the best time to be at the ballpark. One day, Tommy Lasorda is pitching a nine inning "game" to a group of rookies just up from the minors. On another, Mike Scioscia and Fernando Valenzuela are playing home run derby. Everyday, starters and relievers will face each other in a hitting game umpired by one of the coaches.

It is also a time of constant repetition. Hitters hustle in and out of the batting cage. Some call for a specific pitch, some just want to keep their swing sharp. Coaches are banging ground balls to the infielders. Another coach is popping fungoes to the outfielders. Kirk Gibson has a round of stretching exercises he does before every game. Other players are running in the outfield. It seems such chaos, but the pattern of pre-game workouts does not vary much. A quick infield practice will follow the visiting team's batting practice. After this, the Dodgers will go back to their dressing room through their dugout. They will change into fresh game uniforms and be ready for their night's work.

7:30 on a Los Angeles summer night. The stands are rapidly filling. The umpires have rubbed up seven dozen baseballs with "Mississippi Mud" and are walking to their positions. The ball boys are walking down to their chairs on the foul lines. The players are milling in the dugout. Tonight's game will soon begin.

NICK NICKSON

Nick Nickson was looking for a summer job. He is the color commentator on the KLAC broadcasts of the Kings hockey games, so his winter months are busy ones. He has always been a baseball fan and has followed the Dodgers' fortunes ever since moving to Los Angles from New Haven in 1981. The following year, he heard that long-time Stadium announcer John Ramsey, was retiring following the 1982 season. Nickson called the Dodgers to inquire after the job, went in for an audition, won the job and found himself sitting in the press box behind the Stadium microphone at the start of the 1983 season. So he had his summer job.

Nickson likes the contrast between hockey and baseball. The winter sport is all motion and constant action. The summer game is more gradual in its build up, with more intricate strategy. Since his primary duty is to announce each batter, Nickson has plenty of time to mull over the strategy that Tommy Lasorda might be hatching. The tranquility and mental exercise of the ball park is the perfect break after the manic intensity of covering the Kings. Still, after the slower pace of baseball, he is looking forward to describing some more hockey. The two sports dovetail perfectly. The end of each season leaves him looking forward to the start of the other sport.

Nickson gets to the Stadium two hours before game time. He will have dinner in the press dining room and go over the script for tonight's game. This is prepared by the Dodgers marketing and promotions department and outlines any pre-game ceremonies scheduled for the day. After dinner, he will look up the opposition's broadcasters to make sure he has the pronunciation of the players' names correct. He will also ask them if there are any personnel changes on the visiting team.

This type of preparation pays off. Nickson has never had any glaring mistakes in his six seasons as Dodger public address announcer. The worst one he could think of occurred in his second game when he looked down at his scorecard and announced that the catcher, "Steve" Scioscia was coming to bat. It was the last time he wrote down only the last name of any player in his scorecard.

POST-GAME

Even in a close game, some fans start to leave after the seventh inning. After the last out, most of the people still in the Stadium get up to go. But there are always those few bitter enders. Whether they just want to soak up as much of the ambience of the ballpark as possible or just don't want to deal with the congestion sure to be found in the parking lot, they remain in their seats until the ushers move in to start clearing out the area. This sort of fan probably got to the Stadium early to watch batting and infield practice. They will be visible in the parking lot playing catch or tossing a frisbee. The more poetic among them will be in one of the lots above the Pasadena Freeway, savoring the best view in Los Angeles of the Downtown skyline.

As soon as the last of the fans have moved away from their seats and started for their cars, an army of cleaning people descend on the vacated Stadium. They will spend the night sweeping, hauling, hosing, and waxing until the ballpark is spotless and prepared for the next day's onslaught. While the cleanup crew is removing all the trash, Arthur's Foods workers will be stocking up the concession stands. Elsewhere, stock people for Facility Merchandising, Inc. are preparing the vendor stands for tomorrow's game. Down on the field, the grounds crew is doing some minor maintenance on the field. They will return about noon to make sure the playing field is ready for a major league game.

Little of what happens late at night at Dodger Stadium has much drama. It is kin to the constant repetition of batting and infield practice. It seems boring and unbearably repetitive on the surface, but without it the game would not flow smoothly. Tons of trash are hauled out of Dodger Stadium after every home game. The dirt and grass of the playing surface has to be constantly tended or it will adversely effect the game. None of this tends to make the news. But all of it is vital to the operating of the ballpark.

POST-GAME INTERVIEW, DUGOUT

The Dodgers just beat the Braves, 2-0 on a Mike Scioscia home run. As the stands empty and the parking lots fill, the catcher is sitting in the dugout speaking into a radio microphone. Don Drysdale, who now conducts the post-game interview for the English language stations on the Dodger radio network, is sitting to the right of Scioscia. The initial questions will have to do with the home run. The others will deal with the catcher's tender heel and his thoughts about the upcoming National League Championship Series.

Two print journalists are also listening in on the conversation. They may ask a few questions in the dugout once the radio segment is closed, but most of their queries will take place back in the informality of the clubhouse. Television is also more likely to be away from the dugout. The strong lights necessary for video cameras leave harsh shadows behind the subject. They will normally be in the more brightly lit clubhouse or out on the field.

The man sitting to Scioscia's left is Rene Cardenas. He and Jaime Jarrin announce the Dodger games in Spanish. The flagship station for the Spanish language broadcasts is KWKW in Los Angeles. Their signal is bounced off a satellite in order to beam the game to parts of Latin America. The Spanish language network involves even more stations and reaches more people than its English counterpart.

KWKW uses the same format as KABC. Both feature pre- and post-game interviews. But as is the case with the other Spanish language stations covering all of California's major league teams, KWKW's interviews have to be translated. Some of the Dodgers, such as Fernando Valenzuela or Alfredo Griffin, speak the language natively. Others, such as Tommy Lasorda, Mike Scioscia, Steve Sax, and Franklin Stubbs, speak enough to get by. There is also Ron Perranoski who knows eight or nine Spanish phrases and always manages to work them into the conversation. If the guest speaks no Spanish at all, the announcer will simply translate whatever is said. In the event that Rene Cardenas and Don Drysdale are set to speak to the same player after a game, Jaime Jarrin will give scores and recap the game until the English interview is completed. He will then introduce Cardenas and his guest, and they will be heard internationally.

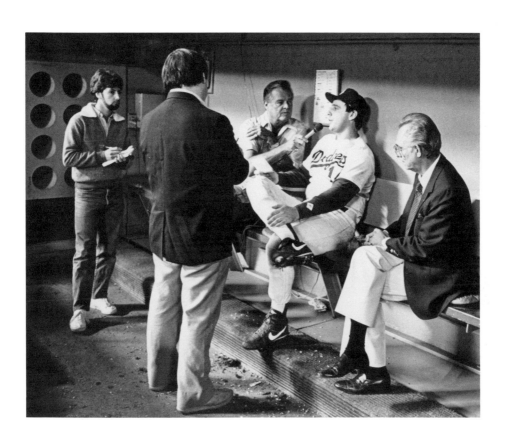

CLUBHOUSE, POST-GAME

The clubhouse after a victory is cheerful chaos. Players are running about in various stages of undress, reporters are crowded around one or more lockers, bat boys are pushing huge carts filled with soiled uniforms toward the washing machine, and in the hall outside, the Dodgers' spikes are being washed in another machine. Tonight the pitching hero was Orel Hershiser and the winning run was knocked in by Mike Marshall. Both of them have reporters gathered around, especially Hershiser. There is even one intrepid woman reporter taking notes as Orel speaks. This is still a fairly rare sight in this most masculine of environments.

Kirk Gibson scored the winning run tonight. He has his share of reporters to deal with. The microphones are from radio reporters who will use the quotes in later broadcasts. Television crews are usually present only late in the season and film often in the clubhouse. This priviledge is denied still photographers who lack official permission from the Dodger front office. Pictures are supposed to only be taken out in the hallway prior to entering the room. Transgressors are brought to the attention of Dave Wright, Dodger clubhouseman, who will explain the rules.

The clubhouse gives players a chance to decorate their cubicle as they see fit. Kirk Gibson has a Michigan State pennant hanging from his. Fernando Valenzuela and Orel Hershiser have pictures of their families tacked up. Micky Hatcher has a helmet with small bobbing baseballs attached by wire on a hook at his locker. Jeff Hamilton's just has his name and number.

Reportedly, it is the comraderie of the locker room that former athletes generally miss the most once they have retired. It is easy to see why. Everyone—reporters, clubhouse men, batboys—are subtly excluded here. There is nothing stated by the players and they are usually willing to cooperate so long as the rules are observed. But far more than the field at batting practice, this is their space, and anyone entering it who is not a player is an outsider.

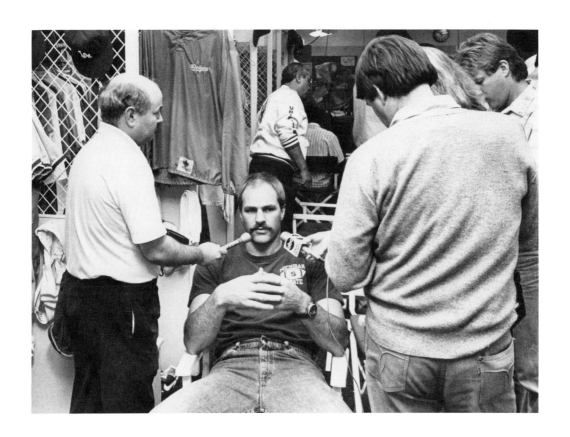

TOMMY LASORDA AND THE AMERICAN IDEAL

The American male ideal has traditionally involved strong, silent men who were self-contained loners bent stoically to a task. Gary Cooper, Humphrey Bogart, John Wayne, Clint Eastwood, and Sylvester Stallone have played the role often in the movies. Sizing up a problem, meeting it head on, solving it with as few words as possible, moving on without thanks when the task was done. Funny, gregarious, witty men sometimes appeared as sidekicks or comic relief. They were never in charge, and rarely to be taken seriously.

This is Tommy Lasorda's problem. Since replacing Walter Alston as Dodger manager in 1977, Lasorda has a .593 winning percentage. His teams have won six Western Division titles, four National League pennants, and two World Championships. In 1988 he was voted Manager of the Year for his role in helping lead the Dodgers to a pennant after two consecutive fifth place finishes. All this success and still it seems hard to take him seriously. Lasorda with his emotionalism, bombasity, and outrageous good humor simply does not fit the Pattonesque stereotype of a sports leader.

To an unusual degree, Lasorda's office reflects the man within. Walter Alston worked out of an unadorned, small space. When Lasorda took the job, he moved to a larger room and immediately started decorating. There is a uniform locker, of course, with a few trophies on it, and a big screen television. The walls are completely covered with photographs and drawings. Both Frank Sinatra and Don Rickles have their own walls. The rest of the space is devoted to ballplayers active and retired, family pictures, and religious messages.

Win or lose, the door is open after a game. A table groans with the post-game meal. Players wander in and out. Newsmen question the manager about the team's performance. The phone rings constantly. Lasorda presides over the proceedings, answering questions, cajoling players, telling jokes and baseball stories. Always talking a mile a minute. Loose, enjoying himself. Not acting anything remotely like John Wayne or Vince Lombardi. Seeming to be every inch the comic relief sidekick, not the main star. But he knows baseball, and his teams win. Why should he be faulted for having so much talent for telling a story?

ON STAGE AND BACKSTAGE WITH THE BATBOYS

My great-uncle, John Connor, was a batboy for the Chicago White Sox and later an umpire in the Class A California League. My childhood was filled with stories of the aggression of Ty Cobb, the kindliness of Walter Johnson, the dominance of Babe Ruth, and the tragedy of Shoeless Joe Jackson. Fifty years after the fact he remembered which kind of tobacco the different players would send him to pick up. Sometime in the mid 2030s Shawn Evans and Pete Sandoval will be sitting with their grandchildren, spinning yarns about the 1988 Dodgers, and their unlikely World Championship.

They are two of the six Dodger batboys. The word is something of a misnomer. Both are men in their early 20s who started working for the Dodgers after playing ball at Pasadena City College. Their direct boss in Nobe Kawano, who has run the Dodger clubhouse ever since the team came west. The day's schedule will call for two men to work in the dugout, two on the foul lines, and two more back in the clubhouse.

Evans prefers the dugout post. Not only are you running around a bit—taking balls to the umpires and getting the bats— but you have a chance to listen to the talk on the bench and get a better insight into the strategy of the game. Working the foul lines is the second best assignment. Here you will play catch with one of the outfielders, shag stray balls, and talk to fans. There can be long pauses between action, however, and April and September nights can be pretty cold at the Stadium.

The night I talked to Pete Sandoval, he had the clubhouse duty. When I walked in right after the game, he already had the first post-game wash going. This is definitely the backstage activity for the batboys. They are responsible for making sure all the ballplayer's washable paraphernalia is collected and popped into the huge washing machine just outside the clubhouse. Persistent stains, such as those caused by sliding on grass, will be taken to Ophelia Grajeda, who works on them until they are gone.

Since players wear one uniform for batting practice and a second for the game, the washing machine has been turning most of the time the Dodgers spent beating the Braves. Pete will be here for another hour. He is up to his elbows in soiled uniforms and undershirts, with more arriving all the time. But no complaints. This is what it takes to be part of the show.

RALPH GARCIA

Ralph Garcia spends most of the game up on the blue level and never pays for his seat. He is the driver of the huge Gray Line bus that transports the visiting team players back and forth between their hotel and the ballpark. Garcia has driven for the company for years, but sees this as the best assignment he's had so far. "I'm a big fan," he says. "This not only gives me the chance to see a lot of games, but I meet lots of the players, too." The only drawback is that the teams are usually lousy tippers.

Much of Garcia's schedule is in the hands of the visiting team's traveling secretary. He will pick which of the downtown hotels the club will use—generally the Biltmore, Hyatt Regency, or Sheraton Grande—and what time the team will leave for the Stadium. The chief variable in departure time from the hotel is whether or not the visitors are going to take batting practice. There is only one bus used on these runs unless it is get away day. Then a second coach will be used to store all the added luggage and equipment. The extra space also helps if the team has lost. Often players will want to be as far away from the managers and coaches as possible.

While Garcia is up on the Reserved Level watching the game, his bus is parked out behind center field. He starts making his way back to work during the eighth inning. When the Dodgers are on the road, Garcia is down south driving visiting American League teams to play the Angels at Anaheim Stadium. But being a Dodger fan of long standing, Ralph prefers working with the National League. So far, the Expos, Braves, and Pirates have been the most fun to be around. Any trip is improved, of course, if the team has won. Then they will leave about an hour after the last out and be loose and joking in the manner of young men everywhere. After a loss, the team is out of the dressing room much more quickly and in a somber mood.

The only other problem Ralph has to deal with is the irrefutable law of nature that buses are never, under any circumstances, to sully the outfield grass. Manuvering one of those behemoths through the center field gate and around the foul line curves is no easy task. Sensing the obvious question, Garcia holds up his hands and says, "With practice, I'm getting better."

GROUNDS CREW

As soon as the last out is recorded the grounds crew goes back to work. The only time they are seen during a game is when the infield is dragged at the top of the fifth inning or if rain necessitates unrolling the tarp. But they are around the park nonetheless. It makes for a long day. The keepers of the field have been at work since before noon.

Al Hicks is fairly new to the Chavez Ravine. Prior to his Los Angeles arrival he worked for the Parks Department at Port Charlotte, Florida, the Texas Rangers, and the Dodgers facility at Vero Beach. He is as happy to be with the big club as Tracy Woodson. Hicks has served his apprenticeship in "sports facilities management." He notes that it is a specialized type of gardening and consists of "a little more than cuttin' the grass and rakin' the dirt."

Tonight, in the dimness of only half the Stadium's lights, Hicks, Al Myers, Rico Rivera, and Vince Vasquez will only cover the batter's boxes and mound with small tarps and lightly water down the field. The real work comes tomorrow, but the watering is important to both keep the playing field green and make sure the plate and mound keep their proper consistency. Hicks points out that hitters hate a soft batter's box. They want to be able to dig in. Likewise, if the mound is too soft the pitchers will dig holes all over it with their spikes since their individual strides can be so different.

The morning will be the time to take the measurements. The outfield grass is cut every day and kept at $5/8$ of an inch. The infield is cut every other day, getting no longer than half an inch. Hicks notes that these lengths can change quite a bit around the league. Teams with slower fielders tend to keep the grass a bit longer to increase drag on the ball and thereby give the glovemen a split second longer to reach a groundball. A nail drag will be used to rip the top half inch of the clay surface of the infield. If this was not done on a daily basis the top of the infield would bake as hard as a brick. Each day one and a half to two hours is spent on the preparation of the infield. The pitcher's mound takes special attention, also. The rubber cannot be higher than ten inches above the plate and the slope of the mound cannot be more than one inch per foot. Once all this work is done, the field is ready for major league baseball.

THE SOUVENIR STAND

It's well over an hour since the conclusion of the game. The Dodgers lost to San Diego tonight, 5-4. Few fans stuck around to try and get an autograph after the bitter loss. Business was not much better at the souvenir stands. Hard losses and extra innings games are awful for the vendors. Their best nights take place after a late inning Dodger victory. Then everyone wants to take something home.

But win or lose, inventory goes on. So, while food supply trams rumbeled by, Ray Kaulig counted pennants, caps, t-shirts, and yearbooks. Also on the list was an item new this year. Umpire cards. Full color cards featuring the thirty-one National League umpires with a $15.00 price tag. The cards were printed by Paul Runge. Proceeds from sales went into a special fund for the umpires. Kaulig noted that the cards sold fairly well for so expensive an item.

Many of the vendor's items are perennials and sell pretty evenly throughout the season. Caps are an example of this, or pennants. Team logo jackets sell better in cold weather, while t-shirts sell better when it is warm. Yearbooks, as you would expect, sell more quickly at the beginning of the year. Every thing sells better when the team is winning, but the percentage of people buying small bats, dolls, or wristbands doesn't seem to change that drastically. A customer in the market for more esoteric items—such as books about the Dodgers or broken bats used by team members—will have to forsake the local souvenir stand for the Dodger Gift Shop. It is open all year long and located on the red level.

The one drawback to a job at the Stadium for a dedicated baseball fan is summed up in Kaulig's comment that he has been to every Dodger game for the past five years but hasn't seen one of them. It drives David Taliaferro nuts to hear the distict roar of a crowd excited by a play or hit as he is making his hot dogs in Annette Saldano's concession stand on the Field Level. Some times when he gets a bit ahead in his hot dog cooking, he takes a moment to run out and see what is happening on the field. Marc Proval thinks this is why being an usher is one of the best jobs in the Stadium. He is almost always in a position to keep one eye on the action. For the same reason, Shawn Evans would rather spend his evening bat-boying from the dugout rather than washing clothes back in the clubhouse. Most of those working at the Stadium are there because it is a good way to make some extra money while indulging their interest in baseball.

THE CLEAN UP CREW

No sooner has Dodger security made sure the last of the fans are moving toward the exits than an army of cleaners descends on the seats. Various parts of the force will work most of the night. When they leave, Dodger Stadium, the third oldest ball park in the National League, will look brand new.

The "sweepers" are the first of the crews to get to work. You can hear them all over the empty Stadium as they pop up the seat bottoms with their brooms to get at the refuse underneath. Adeline Tamez is a supervisor with the sweepers and notes that she generally has about 40 people in her crew. More are brought in when the crowd is larger. During the game they have been sweeping up in the public walkways and making sure the restrooms stay clean. At its conclusion they will sweep all the trash discarded under the seats into the center aisles. The shovel crew moves in at this point to lift the trash into small containers, and eventually to empty these into the larger dumpsters located in the walkways.

Once the sweepers and shovelers have cleared out the trash, the hose team comes in to spray down the seats and aisles. Tonight Samuel Saldana will wash the entire orange level with a high powered hose. Meanwhile, the "mop men" are cleaning the concourse areas in preparation for the arrival of the "deck men" in their tractorized waxing units.

As the cleaning crews go about their business, beer and food trains are making their rounds taking perishables to the Arthur Foods storage space on the blue level and replacing needed nonperishables. Tomorrow, fresh hot dogs and peanuts will arrive at the stands. Beer kegs and soda pop syrup containers will be connected and ready to serve thristy fans.

After every home game it's the same thing. Men and women with brooms, hoses, and shovels remove tons of trash while other workers mop, wax, fill up the food stands, and sweep the parking lots. By the time the first fans start to filter into the park at 6:00 p.m., the place will be so clean it is impossible to tell there was an event held in the Stadium the previous day.

GETAWAY DAY

It's early June and the Dodgers have just split a four game series with the second place Houston Astros. The Dodgers won today. Orel Hershiser beat the all-time strikeout leader in baseball history, Nolan Ryan. The clubhouse is loose. Kirk Gibson has an ice pack on his right knee. He is telling a group of reporters that they should quit worrying so much about all the guys on the Disabled List. "You can't worry about that. We raise each other up. That's what being a team's all about."

Orel Hershiser is at his locker, surrounded by reporters. The right sleeve has been entirely cut off the grey t-shirt he wears under his long-sleeved undershirt. A sweat stain extends all the way down the right side of the shirt. He answers questions from the assembled scribes and accepts congratulations from teammates with the same serious demenor. When the last reporter has asked his questions, Hershiser asks respectfully, "Is that enough?" He finally can take his shower.

Lasorda is holding court in his office. The television is on, the table loaded with food, the reporters ready with their notebooks in hand. The manager looks up to see Steve Sax walk in the office to see what's to eat. "Hey Saxy," he yells, "Look who's on t.v." Sax moves over to where he can see the giant screen. He pauses to watch the Three Stooges awhile. "I love these guys," he says.

Meanwhile, back in the tunnels under the stands the equipment trucks are being loaded. This is a getaway day. Tomorrow night the Dodgers will play the Padres in San Diego. Bats, balls, gloves, uniforms, and hats have to be loaded into bags, carted out to the waiting truck, and driven south down Interstate 5. If the team was headed east, all the equipment would be driven to the airport. Jim Barnhart and his crew will load 4800 pounds worth of Dodger gear this night. And that doesn't even include the luggage each team member will carry with him. Barnhart figures to drive as far as San Onofre, stop and eat some dinner while watching the Laker game, and then press on to San Diego. By 3:30 tomorrow when the players start to arrive at the visitor's clubhouse at Jack Murphy Stadium, they will find their uniforms and equipment laid out and waiting for them. But that's tomorrow. Tonight the truck is still to be loaded.

THE PLAYERS' PARKING LOT

The Dodger team parking lot is reached by walking down a long corridor past the weight room, shower room, and batting cage and then climbing the stairs to a gate located just behind the home team bullpen. Inside the lot, the player will find both his car and several guards. Ringing the chain link fence, and often hanging over it, he will be confronted by fans calling for him to come over and give them an autograph.

The autograph seekers are predominantly male and young. They are noisy and demanding when a player appears, but rarely surly. The kids, of course, are the most energetic. They are the ones precariously hanging over the top of the fence loudly begging whichever Dodger is in the lot to come over and give them a signature. The player will be escorted to his car by one or more of the LAPD or Dodger officers. Whatever abuse comes the player's way is only verbal, and usually not vicious. Gary Hinderaker considers this duty a vacation after some of the problems he has to deal with on his police beat. "At least here we're dealing with decent people."

If the player decides to sign some autographs, he usually does so near his car. Their styles of signing differ markedly. Steve Sax signs for a short time each day. When the time he has set for himself is up, he says, "Gotta go," hops in his car and is gone. Rick Dempsey, reaching the end of his career, and Jeff Hamilton, at the beginning of his, generally ride home together. They sign every night, as do Franklin Stubbs and Mike Scioscia. They are only rarely joined by Jesse Orosco and Mike Marshall. Kirk Gibson prefers to answer autograph requests through the mail.

Don Sutton, a 300 game winning pitcher in the last months of his career, did not mind signing autographs in the least. When asked if he had any idea how many times he had signed something for someone, he said, "No idea. I just keep hoping I get to do it one more time." John Shelby will usually give some autographs. He sees it as part of the game, but notes that the fans in L.A. are a lot more dedicated to getting a signature than those in Baltimore. "They will be out there in the rain or after an extra inning game. Anytime. People in Baltimore wanted to go home." It seems fitting that in the film capital of the world the autograph seekers would not only be more numerous but also more persistent.

THE OBJECT OF THEIR DESIRE

America in the late 20th Century is a nation with few heroes but many idols. Never has the craze for securing the signature of famous people been more manic. Events such as book signings, personal appearances, and premieres are designed to give the public a chance to play a peripheral but immediate part in the lives of the object of their desire. This type of idol worship is hardly unique to the United States, but the open nature of our society and the demands of its democratic myths of equality make Americans particularly insistent on having access to the stars.

Baseball players are the most popular sports figures when it comes to autographs. One of the latest wrinkles in the exploding market for baseball cards is the appearance of both retired and current ballplayers at card conventions. A Mickey Mantle autograph might cost a fan $20 while Wade Boggs signs for $15. At that, the lines are usually long.

Autographs at the Stadium don't cost anything. You will see players writing their names on pictures, cards, and balls as they wait for batting practice or the game to start. Some will sign for fans along the third base line during pregame warmups. Most take a moment at least to work the crowded fence in the player's parking lot after the game. This is usually done doggedly, with an absolute minimum of conversation. Dodgers will usually answer any question directed at them as briefly as possible. There always seems to be someone in any collection of fans that is so lost in the bitterness of their own lack of fulfillment that they can't help but express anger at the favored individual being asked for an autograph. The players have all experienced this a hundred times before. They protect themselves by being cordial, but not friendly. There is always something held in reserve when they are in a crowd of fans.

Whenever it seems the player is about to leave, the plea for "just one more" inevitably starts. "How come you never understand when a guy's got some place to be," asked John Shelby. Not really a question. No answer was offered. But leave they must "Gotta go," says Steve Sax. "My family is waiting for me," says John Shelby. Usually the fans will shout their thanks when it is apparent that the player will sign no more that night. But occasionally you will get a plaintive cry like the one that followed Kirk Gibson into his car one night. A man stood against the fence and wailed over and over, "Kirk, man, you just don't understand!"

No doubt he doesn't.

ENDGAME

It's late at night. The player's parking lot is empty, the policemen guarding it have all gone home. There wasn't much happening out there tonight, anyway. The Dodgers suffered a tough 5-4 loss to the Padres on an eighth inning home run that probably should have been caught. There was plenty of room around the fence, for once. It must have been evident to everyone that tonight was the wrong time to ask for an autograph. Most of the players just walked through the gate leading to the lot and headed directly to their cars, heads down. Very few shouts of "Kirk, Kirk!" or "Steve, Steve!" tonight. About the only ones to do any signing were Rick Dempsey and Jeff Hamilton. Everyone knows it is just a matter of time until the Dodgers clinch the Westen Division title. Tonight did not bring it any closer to home.

Tommy Lasorda was subdued, also. He takes it for granted his team will clinch soon, but this is a man who hates to lose. As always his office is full of people. The gloom of the past two losing seasons is nowhere in evidence, but neither is the ebullience that follows a victory. Lasorda is telling a reporter from Japan that the 1988 Dodgers are better than the past two years is because the gaping holes that have plagued the team were filled during the off season. The manager credits Dodger Vice President Fred Claire for going out and getting the right players to plug the gaps, and President Peter O'Malley for giving him both the go ahead and the funding to get quality players.

The acres of asphalt that surround the Stadium are empty. The fans, players, and vendors have all gone home. The ballpark is only dimly lit as the crews go about their nocturnal rounds. The only sounds in the ravine are the metallic clanking of the beer trains and the whining of the air blowers used to clean the stands. An occasional shout from one of the workers is audible. Otherwise all is silence. It is like seeing "Old Ironsides," the *U.S.S. Constitution*, tied up in Boston Harbor. The sight is beautiful but seems unnatural. Ships should be at sea and ball parks should be full of fans excited by the spectacle before them. Well, at least the freeways aren't crowded this early in the morning. They look great empty.

AFTERWARD: THE VICTORY PARADE

One of the primary attractions of professional sports is its appeal to the thirst for grandeur in people's lives. There is little risk to the fan in the rocky quest for greatness. It is perfectly safe to invest your emotions in a team because the triumphs or failures are all vicarious. Whether your team wins or loses, you will still have the same job, same relationships, same debts.

But even vicarious thrills can be sublime. On October 24, 1988, the World Champion Los Angeles Dodgers were feted with a celebration organized by the city and called "Dodger Day Downtown." The team was transported down Broadway on a series of floats. The destination was the steps of City Hall where the main rally was to take place. In all, over 70,000 people took the chance to share in the Dodgers' triumph.

As the team was being cheered down Broadway, the crowd at City Hall was entertained with a tape of Vin Scully's World Series calls. "Glory Days" and "Center Field" were played over the sound system. When the floats bearing the players pulled up on the Main St. side of City Hall, "I Love L.A." blasted out of the loud speakers. As the Dodgers were working their way to the place of honor, six helicopters circled overhead to record the event for the evening news. Down on the ground, the fans yelled, banners were unfurled, signs lifted high. The crowd reveled in its chance to be a direct participant in celebrating the team's gritty triumph over the Oakland Athletics.

The roll players and the stars all had their time in the sun. Kirk Gibson, Mickey Hatcher, Steve Sax, and the fan's obvious favorite, Orel Hershiser, all spoke briefly to the crowd. Vin Scully narrated the event, Mayor Tom Bradley welcomed everyone, the UCLA cheerleaders frolicked, the Dodger wives were cheered, Tommy Lasorda danced, and the attending politicians had the good sense to just sit and share in the reflected glory.

The disappointing 1986 and 1987 seasons proved conclusively that all the Dodgers have to do is put nine men in blue and white uniforms on the field to draw two million people. The city loves their team. Uncomplicatedly and unequivocally. Fans will show up to see a poor team in great enough numbers, but give them a year long contender and almost three million people will show up at the Stadium.

Given a World Championship to celebrate, 70,000 of those fans happily and non-violently crowded Downtown to express their joy in the Dodgers' triumph—and to share in the grandeur.

A LOS ANGELES BASEBALL BIBLIOGRAPHY

The best source for following baseball in Los Angeles is the daily sports pages of the *Times* and *Herald-Examiner*. The Pacific Coast League was closley covered in the now defunct *Daily News* (whose morgue is available at the UCLA Research Library) and the since merged *Examiner*.

GENERAL

Henstell, Bruce, *Sunshine and Wealth: Los Angeles in the Twenties and Thirties* (San Francisco: Chronicle Books, 1984).

Reidenbaugh, Lowell, *Take Me Out to the Ballpark* (St. Louis: Sporting News, 1983).

Torrence, Bruce T., *Hollywood: The First Hundred Years* (New York: New York Zoetrope, 1982).

Weaver, John D., *Los Angeles: The Enormous Village, 1781-1981* (Santa Barbara: Capra Press, 1980).

PACIFIC COAST LEAGUE

Beverage Richard, *Hollywood Stars: Baseball in Movieland, 1926-1957* (Placentia: Deacon Press, 1984).

— *The Angels: Los Angeles in the Pacific Coast League* (Placentia: Deacon Press, 1981).

Goodale, George, *The Los Angeles Angels Baseball Club and All-Time Record Book* (Los Angeles: Los Angeles Angels Baseball Club, 1951).

Lange, Fred, *History of Baseball in California and Pacific Coast Leagues, 1847-1938* (Oakland: Lange, 1938).

Panella, Bob, "All Eras End—And With Memories," *Hollywood Citizen-News*, March 3, 1958, p.12.

Professional Baseball Parks in the Los Angeles Area (Los Angeles: City of Los Angeles Bicentennial Project, 1981).

Rowe, David G., *Pacific Coast Baseball League Records, 1903-1954* (San Francisco: Pacific Coast Baseball League, 1955).

Schroeder, W.R., *The Pacific Coast League From 1903 to 1940*, (Los Angeles: Helms Athletic Foundation, 1941).

Spink, J.G. Taylor, "Cobb Flings Coast All-Star Challenge," *The Sporting News* (January 14, 1948), p.5.

Zimmerman, Tom, "Before Dodger Stadium," *Dodger Scorecard Magazine* (July, 1987), p.20-21.

118

Finch, Frank, *The Los Angeles Dodgers: The First Twenty Years* (Virginia Beach: Jordan & Co., 1977).

Henderson, Cary S., "Los Angeles and the Dodger War, 1957-1962," *Southern California Quarterly*, v.62 (Fall, 1980), p.261-289.

Hines, Thomas S., "Housing, Baseball, and Creeping Socialism: The Battle of Chavez Ravine, Los Angeles, 1949-1959," *Journal of Urban History*, v.8 (February, 1982), p.123-143.

Los Angeles Dodgers, *Media Guide* (Los Angeles: Dodgers, printed annually, 1958-1988).

Poulson, Norris, *Memoirs*, Oral History Project, Special Collections: University of California at Los Angeles.

Sullivan, Neil J., *The Dodgers Move West* (New York: Oxford University Press, 1987).

Wood, Bob, *Dodger Dogs to Fenway Franks: The Ultimate Guide to America's Top Baseball Parks* (New York: McGraw-Hill, 1988).

Zimmerman, Paul, *The Los Angeles Dodgers* (New York: Coward-McCann, 1960).

Zimmerman, Tom, "Ballparks of Summers Past," *California Living*, (*Los Angeles Herald-Examiner*), March 15, 1987, p.1, 6-11.

ABOUT THE AUTHOR

Tom Zimmerman is a native of Los Angeles. He is completing his Ph.D. in American History at UCLA, where his dissertation topic is the history of photography in Los Angeles. Zimmerman's word and photo essays have appeared in a number of publications, including the *Los Angeles Times Magazine, Americana, Traveler Magazine*, and *The Journal of the West*. His photographs have been exhibited across the country, and are in the permanent collections of the Brooklyn Museum, Dirctor's Guild, California Historical Society, and the Historic American Building Survey at the National Archives.